God Exists
Why
Christianity?

GW00375224

Author

Samuel Miller

Introduction

It has become a basic assumption of Western society that science has displaced theism; it's in our education, it's on the internet and it's on the news. As of 2021 agnosticism/atheism is the third biggest religion.[1] In the UK where I live, we are taught about Humanism in school from the age of 5 and we continue to learn about it throughout secondary school.[2] However, there are more people who claim to believe in the 'Jedi Knight religion' than Humanism (in the UK). According to the 2001 census approximately 400,000 people believe in the Jedi Knight Religion[3], whereas the Humanist UK website claims 100,000 members.[4]

Many people I know don't really care about which religion is true so they are atheists without putting any thought into it, even though it is the biggest dilemma they will ever face. If they pick the wrong religion, they **could** end up spending an eternity in Hell which is worse than the worst thing we can imagine! It is a serious problem that we are heading towards a world where we don't care about eternity. What we care about is self-indulgence in the present. But there are also people who do put thought into the eternal questions of life and still think that atheism is the way. I often see people claim this and defend it with science but as I am going to explain in this book, atheism can't be defended by science.

It is not a Schrödinger's equation where God could exist, but he might not. In fact, he must exist.

It is easy to think that this is a war of science vs religion when we hear great scientists like Stephen Hawking say, "There's no possibility of God existing because time didn't exist before the Big Bang."

Stephen Hawking does not truly understand the nature of God. God is outside of our universe and isn't constricted by time.

Also, remember it is not like all scientists are atheists, although many suggest that this is the case. According to futurity.org 45% of scientists who live in the United Kingdom are atheists.[5] So, using basic logic, the other 55% are agnostics or theists.

Many of the best scientists believed in a creator God (the first 4 in this list were Christians); Isaac Newton[6], James Maxwell[7], Michael Faraday[8], Charles Babbage[9], Albert Einstein[10], Thomas Edison[11], Max Planck[12], Charles Darwin[13] and the list goes on.

"Everyone who is seriously involved in the pursuit of science becomes convinced that some spirit is manifest in the laws of the universe, one that is vastly superior to that of man." – Albert Einstein[14]

"The more I study science, the more I believe in God" – Albert Einstein[15]

Blaise Pascal – who helped develop probability theory - brought up a philosophical argument called Pascal's Wager that is worth considering. If you are a Christian and your God exists you get to heaven, if he doesn't, nothing happens. If you are an atheist and God doesn't exist nothing happens if he does then you go to Hell.

Christians lose nothing at worst or at best gain something, but by being an atheist you are only losing out. You aren't benefiting yourself. In the words of the lottery advert, "You've got to be in it to win it!"

Of course Christians can still end up Hell bound if it turns out that they've picked the wrong God, but chapter 5 talks about other religions and chapter 6 points to the overwhelming historical evidence for the Christian God.

My aim with this book is not to ask people to make a blind leap of faith in a God that they don't know. My hope is that by taking a look at the arguments for and against a creator God and then looking at the evidence for and against the various descriptions of God, more people will make an informed decision rather than accepting dogmatically the prevailing wisdom that science has killed God and the evidence points against Christianity.

Chapters

Chapter 1: Genesis, How was the universe made?

One of the biggest holes in the atheist world view is how they think the universe got here. How did we get something from nothing? If I went and asked someone on the streets, "How do you think the universe was made?"

Chances are their response would be, "I don't know" or "The Big Bang".

That is fair since even top scientists don't know. Something can't be made out of nothing without supernatural interference, let alone a universe with physical constants and laws set perfectly so not only the universe won't implode on itself, but it can even accommodate complex lifeforms such as ourselves. Richard Dawkins (the leading new atheist scientist, author of *The God Delusion*) has *faith* that a scientist will someday work out how the universe was created:

"The universe looks very designed, but it's not designed... The cosmos hasn't yet had its Darwin, we don't yet know how it came into existence."[1]

But he also claims that faith, what he defines as belief without evidence, is one of the world's greatest evils.[2]

Also keep in mind, the Big Bang did not create the universe, it is a name given to the rapid *expansion* of the universe at the beginning of time.

Well, we know the Big Bang did happen due to the Cosmic Background Radiation.[3] But what caused the Big Bang?

The first law of thermodynamics states that energy cannot be created or destroyed, only transferred. But if we track back energy, we eat a cow, the cow eats grass, the grass gets energy from the Sun, and it can go all the way back to

11

the Big Bang, but why was enough energy to cause the Big Bang spontaneously created?

The Big Bounce theory says the universe has always existed, a big bang happens, it inflates, it deflates under its own gravitational pull (a Big Crunch), it is an infinite loop. Imagining this is the case, we could have infinite more universes ahead of us in theory, but still even that would still have a first universe. This doesn't get us closer to answering the question, "Where did the universe come from?" it just shoves it under the rug. I could just believe the whole world is a virtual reality in some other universe, but I have no reason to believe that. It is not an argument against a created universe, I see it as a philosophy for a Deistic God. This view has also been rejected by almost all serious scientists since the early 1980s after inflationary cosmology emerged. The second law of thermodynamics also prohibits perpetual motion machines (like the universe if the Big Bounce was true).

Stephen Hawking in his book *The Grand Design* says the time before the universe was a perfect vacuum, but I suggest it was truly nothing. The difference here is important because he then goes on to say that because of quantum mechanics and relativity the universe will create itself from nothing.

At the end of his book, he claims,

"Because there is a law such as gravity, the universe can and will create itself from nothing. Spontaneous creation is the reason there is something rather than nothing, why the universe exists, why we exist. It is not necessary to invoke God to light the blue touch paper and set the universe going."[4]

Well first of all, there's a contradiction there, he says because there is a law such as gravity the universe will create itself from nothing. It isn't nothing if there is a law of gravity, is it? But ignoring that I still have some questions.

How did the universe actually get there in the first place, how did the vacuum originally get there with the laws of physics? Saying 'the universe just is and that is all there is to it' is incoherent. Furthermore, even if there was a quantum fluctuation that somehow created the universe out of nothing it couldn't create this much energy, the universe is still expanding 13.8 billion years after the Big Bang happened!

But a bigger problem is, the book attempts to explain how a universe such as ours can be created from quantum mechanics but he doesn't explain why quantum mechanics is there in the first place, in another universe why would it need QM? It can't be a starting point for creating a universe from 'nothing'. You need to start *before* a vacuum.

In the words of Dr John Lennox 'Nonsense remains nonsense, even when talked by world-famous scientists.'

The second law of thermodynamics states that every irreversible process in a closed system will increase the entropy (disarray) of the system. Most atheists believe the Big Bang was an irreversible process, they also by definition believe the universe is a closed system without outside interaction. But if that is the case, our existence would not make sense. Evolution is an example of the universe becoming more ordered. Why did the universe start with such low entropy?

A very strong argument for a designed universe is 'fine tuning'. Paul Davies said, "There is now broad agreement among physicists and cosmologists that the Universe is in several respects 'fine-tuned' for life". Sir Fred Hoyle, a secular astronomer, when he discovered what was required to produce just the right conditions for the preponderance of carbon as a basis of life, he said "nothing shook my atheism more". His calculations suggested that acquiring the required number of enzymes for the simplest cell would be 1 in $10^{40,000}$.[5] This number is considerably greater than the number of seconds that have known to have passed in the universe so far multiplied by the number of atoms in the universe. Stephen Hawking said "The laws of science, as we know them at present, contain many fundamental numbers ... The remarkable fact is that the values of these numbers seem to have been very finely adjusted to make possible the development of life." Roger Penrose calculated the chances of the fine tuning of the initial entropy of the universe to be (10^{10})^123, that number is 1 followed by 1.23 *trillion* zeros[6], that is inconceivable! Writing 1 zero a second, that would take 39,000 years.

According to Paul Davies, if the strong nuclear force were 2% stronger than it is already, and the other physical constants were left unchanged this would drastically alter the physics of stars. Hydrogen would fuse so easily that it is likely that all the universe's hydrogen would be consumed in the first few minutes after the Big Bang.

Lots of atheists then argue for the multiverse theory because of this. The multiverse theory argues that there isn't a designer, there is just an infinite, or a huge number of universes that we can't access, and because there are so many of course there is one that exists (ours), which has perfectly tuned constants that happens to suit humanity.

But there are problems with this. First, it's a violation of Occam's Razor[7], we have reason to believe in a God but no reason to believe in an infinite of universes that we can't access. Or an even sharper razor, Alder's Razor (also known as Newton's Flaming Laser Sword) states "In its weakest form it says that we should not dispute propositions unless they can be shown by precise logic and/or mathematics to have observable consequences. In its strongest form it demands a list of observable consequences and a formal demonstration that they are indeed consequences of the proposition claimed."[8] This rules the multiverse out as unscientific. To be empirically tested, we would require access to these other universes, which would mean there would be infinite people killing you right now from different universes. God does pass this test. I talk about evidence for God actually showing himself to us through Jesus' resurrection in Chapter 6. The multiverse theory is also guilty of the inverse gambler's fallacy.[9] Using Ian Hacking's example, imagine you walk into a room and see a gambler roll a double six, this is unlikely so you come to the conclusion he must have rolled multiple times before you walked into the room. But this is a fallacy since luck doesn't have memory.

I see a phone and think "Ah, designed by engineers at Samsung." I don't think "Since there are enough planets there will eventually be a random phone that pops into existence." You won't even find a random transistor.

It has also been pointed out that the multiverse theory is unscientific because if it is true, there are infinite universes that are Boltzmann Brains (a brain that spontaneously and briefly popping into existence in a void with fake memories planted in it) and we could be one of them so we can't trust ourselves thinking we are in a multiverse.[10]

Furthermore, the multiverse theory isn't even a viable answer to the fine-tuning problem anyway as Stephen Meyer pointed out in his book *The Return of the God Hypothesis*, both the string-theory model of the multiverse and the inflationary model of the multiverse require more prior fine-tuning than it sets out to solve.[11]

Paul Davies pointed out that if there are infinite universes that must mean there are infinite universes being simulated inside of universes, meaning it is more likely to live in a simulated universe (since the infinite amount of simulated universes will simulate infinite more universes, contrary to an infinite amount of normal universes) so the theory has ultimately leads to a creator God.[12] Along with this, how do we know our universe wasn't simulated a few seconds ago with implantations of fake memories (like Boltzmann brains)?

Atheists also sometimes believe in the Anthropic principle saying the universe is not fine-tuned and the universe has nothing special about it because if the universe could not accommodate intelligent observers, then there would be no one there to observe it. This is a misunderstanding of probability though, since the fact we *can* observe the universe means that it was fine-tuned. The most likely thing is that an intelligent observer wouldn't exist. if I enter the lottery, you could argue it's not 1 in 100,000 if won because 100,000 people are entering and one must win but that's a misunderstanding, since while the universe could have had the physical laws tuned differently the chances it was like this and could produce life is so incredibly rare it shouldn't have happened.

According to quantum cosmology, before Planck time (1^{-43} of a second) the universe was in a superposition of states.[13] The Copenhagen Interpretation (the most popular interpretation of quantum mechanics), says for a wave function to collapse it needs an observer. Does this mean that there was an observer (God?) at the beginning of time, collapsing the universal wave function?

Atheism is a logical fallacy. The world spontaneously popped into existence 13.8 billion years ago, but why that time? Why not earlier? Why didn't the Big Bang happen twenty billion years ago? If something could pop out of nothing, the Big Bang would have happened an immeasurable amount of time ago not at a specific time. How did it go from nothing to something? Why is there a universe instead of no universe? Why is the universe like this? And why are there physical laws instead of chaos?

Ex Nihilo Nihil Fit – From nothing comes nothing. The atheist says, 'from nothing comes everything'.

But even if you do think it is possible for something to come from nothing by a natural process that we haven't discovered yet, even that ultimately leads to God.

Science is showing that the universe is going to come to an end. So, then there will eventually be nothing again. But why can't something come from nothing again if it did before? If something could come from nothing it would since time wouldn't exist. Another universe would pop up after ours. And once that universe popped into existence it would eventually end, another universe pops up and it would go on ad infinitum.

So, if something can come from nothing, that means there are infinite universes. This brings up the problem Paul Davies pointed out with the multiverse (see Page 20-21). If there are infinite universes, infinite things can happen, and in infinite universes a civilization will become so advanced they will be able to simulate another universe inside of their universe, and infinite of those simulated universes will be able to simulate a universe and so on ad infinitum.

It's a basic matter of probability. If there are infinite universes, which there would be if something could come from nothing, there is a 100% chance we are in a simulation with a creator God.

I find it disappointing that so many people come up with foolishness because they can't bring themselves to accept there is a God.

But those aren't the only questions. How did life emerge? You might say, "Evolution", but Darwin's theory of evolution doesn't explain how life originated[14], although I think we probably will find a naturalistic explanation for the origins of life eventually. Fundamentally, Darwinism says the less capable will die because they won't live to breed but the more advanced will survive and reproduce allowing their genes to spread. But that only explains how things change over time, it doesn't explain how life first originated, another vastly important question scientists can't answer.

How did consciousness arise? Evolution doesn't explain that either[15], and I don't think we will ever be able to understand how it arose without God because consciousness isn't (wholly) a material phenomenon as I explain in Chapter 3. Scientists don't know the answer to any of these questions (yet) and way more! They don't even know why a cup will fall to the ground. How does gravity work? Contrary to popular belief, scientists can't explain gravity.[16]

Science views the world around us and describes it, it doesn't *explain* it.

Genesis 1 explains all our creation questions. It first says God created the heavens and the earth. God created the universe. It then says God created the seas. The Earth did indeed used to be an uninhabited water world, 4 billion years ago.[17] It then says God created vegetation: seedbearing plants and trees. Plants did come before *complex* animals, I say complex because there were already simple organisms but would not look like animals as we know them today. Land plants are about 470 million years old[18], but sea plants are one billion years old[19], predating the oldest animal. It then says God created the creatures of the sea. Which is also true, they came before land animals. The first *complex* sea creature was 558 million years ago.[20] Next it says God created animals that moved along land and then he made mankind in his own image. That is also true, 428 million years ago was the first land creature[21] and modern humans are less than quarter of a million years old.

This answers all the big questions, how the universe got here, how life first came about and how consciousness was formed since we were made in God's image (metaphorically, we are creative like God and are able to have a deep awareness like God).

But there are still some problems here, we know the world was made over 13 billion years ago and its creation didn't span over 1 week!

There are a few theories to explain this, but I will cover two that seem most helpful. The first is called 'gap theory'. This suggests that there is no point in thinking the days are consecutive. The creation events described as days took place at various different points in time perhaps spread over billions of years.

The second theory is the 'day age view' which says each day could be long ages of millions to billions of years. I find this view interesting as I think the Bible conveys 7 as a perfect and near infinite number

See Matthew 18:21-22 it says,

"Then Peter came up and said to him, 'Lord, how often shall my brother sin against me, and I forgive him? As many as **seven times**?' Jesus said to him, 'I do not say to you **seven times**, but **seventy times seven**.'"

The use of the number seven in this conversation is similar to the use in these passages, (Gen 4:15), (Gen 4:24), (Ps 119:164), (Prov 24:16) and the Book of Revelation.[22]

Seven seems like a significant number in Hebrew culture and it was common to speak in parables and use numerology, so the author of Genesis might be saying, "This took a long time, maybe billions of years not just 7 days."

People have also pointed out, God experiences time different to us (Psalm 90:4; 2 Peter 3:8), and the Hebrew word for day 'yom' doesn't necessarily mean day, it can also mean a long period of time.

Also, it needs to be said that we aren't changing the Bible around just because it seems to be incompatible with science. The Bible is meant to be interpreted, the early church fathers didn't actually espouse the view that the earth was made in a week and they didn't have geology or evolutionary biology to influence them. Augustine of Hippo believed the world was created instantly and believed that the number seven and six were perfect numbers which, as well as the days, represented something we can't understand[23], he also talked about theistic evolution![24] Irenaeus thought the days were long epochs of time.[25] And many others didn't espouse the view of six-day creationists, even without modern science.

We treat Genesis 1 as a physics textbook at our peril. Genesis 1 is a Middle Eastern theological creation narrative. It follows the "epic" genre of writing typical in Sumeria, Babylonia, and Mesopotamia.[26] The questions it sets out to answer are questions about the nature of God – creator, benevolent, omniscient, omnipotent, eternal and outside of creation.

We need to remember that although the Bible is *for* us, it was not written *to* us. Genesis was written to the ancient Hebrews in a way they would understand. Like Jesus spoke to the people of his time in a way they would understand. But that doesn't mean people from all of time can read it and understand it.

The text is not attempting to answer our modern scientific questions, but universal theological questions.[27] Like Galileo Galilei said, "The Bible shows the way to go to heaven, not the way the heavens go."

"There is no logical reason why nature should have a mathematical subtext in the first place. And even if it does, there is no obvious reason why humans should be capable of comprehending it... Other animals observe the same natural phenomena as we do, but alone among the creatures on this planet, *homo sapiens* can *explain* them"
– Paul Davies[28]

"I do not believe that any scientist who examined the evidence would fail to draw the inference that the laws of nuclear physics have been deliberately designed with regard to the consequences they produce inside the stars."
– Sir Fred Hoyle[29]

Chapter 2: Who created God and how can miracles happen?

Surprisingly, I often hear people ask the question "If the universe has a creator, who created the creator?"

Surely if God has the power to create this universe, to imagine all the colours, all the animals from the mosquito to the T-rex, design the dazzling clusters of galaxies, then God *must* be somewhat unique. God is outside of our universe, so he doesn't have to follow our universe's rules. He is eternal, omnipotent, and omniscient, nothing inside of the universe has these qualities, the laws of thermodynamics make it an impossibility. But don't you think, if he is outside of our universe and is all powerful, he doesn't need to follow our universe's rules? Remember, this is his creation. The creator of a video game isn't limited to the rules of the programming language he has used when he is in real life. A creator is free to have a life outside of his creation.

Suggesting that because the universe needs a creator, the creator must have a creator is guilty of the composition fallacy

If the Bible described a created god, we might have a problem but that is not the case,

Isaiah (43:10): "Before me no god was formed, nor will there be one after me."

Psalms (90:2): "You have always been God—long before the birth of the mountains, even before you created the earth and the world."

Revelation (22:13): "I am the Alpha and the Omega, the First and the Last, the Beginning and the End."

Isaiah (44:6) "This is what the LORD says—Israel's King and Redeemer, the LORD Almighty: I am the first and I am the last; apart from me there is no God."

The other thing I often hear is, 'How can Jesus have performed miracles', or 'He was just a good man; it would have been impossible even for God'.

But surely, if God had created water, could He not walk on it or turn it to wine? David Hume, an 18th century philosopher says that you can't believe in religion because miracles would violate the laws of nature.[1] I disagree, using a similar analogy to earlier, imagine you created a virtual reality, you could just open the console window and run commands/edit the code while playing – of course you could do stuff that would be out of the ordinary for the game like walking on water or even flying that no other players could do if you were the designer or operator of it.

"To use an illustration based on one offered by C.S. Lewis, on each of two nights, if I put ten pounds (British currency) into my drawer, the laws of arithmetic tell me I have twenty pounds. If, however, on waking up I find only five pounds in the drawer I don't conclude that the laws of arithmetic have been broken but possibly the laws of England. The laws of nature describe to us the regularities on which the universe normally runs. God, who created the universe with those laws, is no more their prisoner than the thief is prisoner of the laws of arithmetic. Like my room, the universe is not a closed system, as the secularist maintains." – Dr John Lennox[2]

It is outside interference. Hence, if God created this world, why can't he interfere and change something.

Miracles aren't natural or we would be accustomed to them.

Chapter 3: Does evolution disprove Christianity?

First it is important to explain what evolution is because so many people have strange and unhelpful ideas about it. We all have genes (units of DNA), and our genes can vary through different methods, mainly random mutation. Different genes provide different capabilities. If you walk off a cliff and die you won't be able to breed but if you live long enough to reproduce your genes will carry on so your mutation will spread. Evolution doesn't 'design' stuff, it simply allows interesting stuff to manifest through accidents.

Lots of people think Christianity and other Abrahamic religions can't be true because in the book of Genesis it says Adam and Eve were the first human beings. I don't see a problem here, apes were evolving and eventually evolved into early homo sapiens, but they still weren't properly conscious.

How did consciousness come into place just from *random* mutations (that let me remind you come into place through *mistakes* and are random, famous examples of mutations are down syndrome & colour blindness).

It didn't. Consciousness is so complicated it couldn't have been any amount mutations. As a programmer I can tell you that even if we got an imaginary team of the best programmers possible and we programmed an AGI (artificial general intelligence) even that wouldn't be conscious, it would just emulate consciousness and it wouldn't have creativity. A chess AI is just mindlessly following its code, it can't actually think. Consciousness can actually think, have a deep understanding for little squiggles, imagine complicated structures, speak, be creative and have fun.

We are not simply some chemical reactions that came in by mistake, we are designed.

"Eventually, I believe, current attempts to understand the mind by analogy with man-made computers that can perform superbly some of the same external tasks as conscious beings will be recognized as a gigantic waste of time." – Thomas Nagel[1]

Charles Darwin (creator of theory of natural selection) saw another problem.

"But then with me the horrid doubt always arises whether the convictions of man's mind, which has been developed from the mind of the lower animals, are of any value or at all trustworthy. Would any one trust in the convictions of a monkey's mind, if there are any convictions in such a mind?"[2]

If you believe there is no God and evolution created consciousness alone then you're contradicting yourself.

It is like saying 'This statement is false'. If it is true, then it is false which means it is true and so on. If an unguided process created us, how can we trust our brains to be correct in coming up with the theory?

Evolution does not explain the origins of consciousness by itself.

Evolution doesn't disprove God; it points to God. Have there been hundreds of thousands of very lucky mutations that have led up to creating eyes, ears, stomachs, all of these intricate body parts? Surely it is more likely that there is a force (God) helping evolution go forward because the universe was designed from the beginning.

The chance of a minimally complex cell forming randomly by chance is 1 in 10^40,000. 10^40,000 is massive, bigger than the number of all the subatomic particles (10^{80}) in the observable universe times all the seconds (10^{17}) that has ever passed! I can make it crazier.

The smallest distance in the universe is called Planck length, there are 6.25×10^{34} Planck lengths in a meter (a quick comparison for scale: 1 Planck length to an atom is the same as 1 atom to the solar system!), the diameter of the universe in meters is 8.8×10^{26}, we then see how many Planck lengths are in the diameter of the universe, $(6.25 \times 10^{34}) \times (8.8 \times 10^{26})$ which is 5.5×10^{61}, now cubed so we can find the number of Planck volumes in the universe is 1.6×10^{185}. The smallest amount of time possible is called Planck time. There is 5.39×10^{44} Planck time in a second. 4.36×10^{17} seconds have ever passed in the universe[3], so the amount of Planck time that has ever passed $(4.36 \times 10^{17}) \times (5.39 \times 10^{44})$ is 2.35×10^{62}. Now if we times all the Planck time to have ever passed by all the Planck volumes in the universe $(2.35 \times 10^{62}) \times (1.6 \times 10^{185})$ we get 3.91×10^{247} – not even nearly 10^40000! Let me try and explain what this number is then – if we could somehow make an attempt every moment since the universe began in every Planck volume of the universe rolling the chances, we would have by now had time for roughly 10^{247} attempts, keep in mind life started over 3 billion years ago so when it started it was even more unlikely. Most mathematicians agree that the vanishing point of improbability is 10^50, 10^40000 number is significantly higher than that.[4]

How did the genetic instruction set programmed into DNA come into existence? Even if RNA or DNA arose somehow, they would not contain any genetic instructions unless each nucleotide selection in the sequence was programmed for a function.

"What are the chances that a tornado might blow through a junkyard containing all the parts of a 747, accidentally assembling them into a plane, and leave it ready for take-off? The possibilities are so small as to be negligible even if a tornado were to blow through enough junkyards to fill the whole universe!" – Fred Hoyle[5]

"The existence of mind in some organism on some planet in the universe is surely a fact of fundamental significance. Through conscious beings the universe has generated self-awareness. This can be no trivial detail, no minor byproduct of mindless, purposeless forces. We are truly meant to be here." – Paul Davies[6]

"Whatever one may think about the possibility of a designer, the prevailing doctrine – that the appearance of life from dead matter and its evolution through accidental mutation and natural selection to its present forms has involved nothing but the operation of physical law – cannot be regarded as unassailable. It is an assumption governing the scientific project rather than a well-confirmed scientific hypothesis." – Thomas Nagel[7]

I estimate Adam and Eve were about 12,000-14,000 years ago, this would make sense since it was around then civilization started - the earliest major city we have discovered is the city of Uruk, settled in 4500BC.[8] Agriculture first popped up about 12,000 years ago.[9] The first written languages were Sumerian and Egyptian from 3200BC[10]. All the first cities were founded in the last 12,000 years which fits in well with Adam and Eve. The Garden of Eden was in Mesopotamia[11] (modern day Iraq, which is in West Asia), the Neolithic Revolution originated in West Asia[12] and all of the first civilizations were in Mesopotamia.[13] Humanity have made a great leap forward in terms of language, civilization, and consciousness in the last 12,000 years.

But would Adam and Eve being that recent fit in with the other people mentioned in the Bible? Well if we go to Noah's flood, Adam and Eve being 12,000-14,000 years ago makes sense. Noah was about 1500 years after Adam and

Eve[14], so that must mean sometime in the last 12,500 years there was a massive flood. This was the case, towards the end of the last ice age, which ended 11,000 years ago, there were massive floods due to melting glaciers.[15] So Adam and Eve being 12,000-14,000 years ago adds up with Noah as well.

It also adds up with Cain and Abel. The Bible says Abel was a farmer and Cain was a farmer (Genesis 4:2-4). Farming didn't begin until 12,000 years.[16]

To outline my theory, homo sapiens already existed but didn't have the same level of consciousness as we do until God finally breathed into them and created Adam and Eve. So, Adam and Eve weren't descendants of earlier humans, rather humans were finally ready to reflect God's image upon them so God created completely new humans (Adam and Eve) with the same anatomy. But where is the mention of the 'early' homo sapiens in the

Bible? How come Adam and Eve didn't meet them?

See (Genesis 4:14-15) "Today you are driving me from the land, and I will be hidden from your presence; I will be a restless wanderer on the earth, and **whoever** finds me will kill me.' But the Lord said to him, 'Not so; **anyone** who kills Cain will suffer vengeance seven times over.' Then the Lord put a mark on Cain so that no one who found him would kill him."

For people who don't know, Adam and Eve had 2 kids (at this point) and so far they are the only humans mentioned. Cain just killed his younger brother Abel and God punished him.

By Cain saying 'whoever' it suggests he is not talking about an animal, the same when God says 'anyone'. It could be that they are talking about Adam and Eve but wouldn't Cain then say 'my parents will kill me'? Or maybe he's talking about descendants *to* be born, but if that was the case wouldn't he say, 'my family will kill me' or 'if my parents have any more kids, they will kill me'? Seeing as humans with the same anatomy existed and Cain mentioned other people but weren't Adam and Eve or their descendants it seems that those verses were talking about the 'early homo sapiens'.

Chapter 4: Why is humanity so important?

If we zoom out for a moment it seems self-centred and foolish to think that God created the entire world with us in mind – some animals on a little speck of dust in this massive universe that is so big we can't even observe it all. For all we know, aliens are probably sitting there thinking God created it all for them as well, aren't they?

Let me preface: Aliens almost certainly don't exist. Don't you think it is strange that we haven't had evidence of alien life yet? Given that life is meant to have spontaneously popped into existence on our little planet that isn't even the biggest planet in our solar system, it should be a statistical certainty that aliens exist out there and we might have expected some intelligent ones to have come to us. We have been sending radio signals out into space for over 100 years[1] and these intelligent neighbours have had billions of years to emerge and become superior to us given the size and age of the universe. However, we have seen no evidence of intelligent life, even on the thousands of planets that look fit for intelligent life forms such as ourselves.[2]

Maybe it is because they are really far away and just haven't discovered us yet? Well to that I want to ask how life popped up on their planet. We see some squiggles on a piece of paper and straight away presume it's a sign of intelligent life. Why then when we see life form, then evolve creating a human genome with 6.4 *billion* characters,[3] (1000 times more than the entire Harry Potter series) we presume it is a freak of nature.

No one can understand how life came into place in the first place, it was so unlikely to happen that it couldn't have happened by accident (to evolve into complex life makes it even more unlikely let alone conscious intelligent life), it must have had a creator and couldn't happen again. If God did create us, it would explain why we haven't found aliens in such statistically likely places, and it would explain why we haven't had alien visitors come to us. Palaeontologists, Peter Douglas Ward[4], Donald Brownlee[5], George Gaylord Simpson[6], and Biologists, Ernst Mayr[7] and Theodosius Dobzhansky[8] all reject the possibility of finding alien life due to the statistical improbability.

"Life on Earth was created by a very rare chance of producing a long RNA polymer. Most likely, Earth is the only planet harbouring life in the observable universe." – Professor Totani[9]

I think the only way extra-terrestrial life could exist is if God intervened to put it there, which could in theory be the case since the Bible doesn't say aliens don't exist.

The second thing I want to cover in this chapter is, if we are mere animals, then we are pretty meaningless. We don't have much purpose and we are going to die one day and be forgotten. The Bible however says something different.

Genesis 1:26 "Then God said, 'Let us make mankind in our image, in our likeness, so that they may rule over the fish in the sea and the birds in the sky, over the livestock and all the wild animals, and over all the creatures that move along the ground.'"

Humans were made separately to the animals, animals were made Genesis 1:20-25. It also says man was made in the *image of God* (we can have conscious thought) and we have dominion over animals.

Genesis 9:3 *"Everything that lives and moves about will be food for you. Just as I gave you the green plants, I now give you everything."* Genesis 2:18,20 "The LORD God said, 'It is not good for the man to be alone. I will make a helper suitable for him.' ... [20] So the man gave names to all the livestock, the birds in the sky and all the wild animals."

These verses suggest that animals were made for us as companions and helpers. Our naming of them was a sign of superiority and we are allowed to eat them but not eat humans. We are clearly intended to be distinct from animals. All this leaves out the obvious fact that animals lack consciousness.

"It may be romantic to ascribe human qualities to critters, but it's not very realistic. While animals are by no means dumb, they don't think the same way we do. Contrary to what many popular television shows would have us believe, animals have neither the "theory-of-mind" capabilities that humans have (that is, they are not conscious of what others are thinking) nor the capacity for higher-level reasoning." – Ethologist, Clive Wynne[10]

I think both Christians and Atheists can agree that we need to maintain the distinction. New Atheist thinker, Christopher Hitchens said "Animal rights have been overdone especially when people object to medical experiments".[11] China has gone as far as banning the use anthropomorphic animals in TV programmes to ensure children don't become confused about animal sentience.

There is also the 'observer effect' a hotly discussed topic in quantum physics which implies an important role for observation. When an atomic particle is acting with quantum uncertainty like a wave, it will continue like this until it is observed at which point the wave collapses into a single point like a particle. There is controversy what causes the wave collapse. This has been dubbed the 'measurement problem of quantum mechanics'.

Physicist Fritjof Capra claimed "The crucial feature of atomic physics is that the human observer is not only necessary to observe the properties of an object but is necessary even to define these properties."[12] I am sceptical of whether a human is needed or just any animal can collapse the wave, but if his claim is true then that will mean humans certainly have a fundamental meaning in the universe.

Don't you find it weird when people think that birds flying around, or dolphins swimming is natural but us sitting at home watching TV or texting on a phone isn't natural? Haven't we have just evolved to sit at home and watch TV - whether it's good or not is a different thing - because we are natural creatures as well but if we are just an animal or a freak of nature suggesting things, we do aren't natural is suggesting we are special. Just the fact we say things humans do isn't natural is us noticing that we are special.

Like I have heard several vegetarians/vegans say 'we are just animals too so we shouldn't eat animals'. But if we are just animals it makes sense we can eat other animals since other animals eat each other and it is how 'nature' and the food chain works - we are omnivores. Suggesting we shouldn't eat other animals while we are omnivores is recognising humanity's uniqueness.

Chapter 5: What about other religions?

I often hear people say that religion is silly because how can people claim one is right when there are so many? This makes sense, I could just make one up right now and if I tried hard enough, I could probably properly convince a few people. Does that disprove Christianity? Well let's have a look at some of the top religions and we will see, they have some significant problems.

According to Pew Research the religions by adherents are (not including religions I won't cover such as Folk Religion or Ethnic Religions):[1]

1. Christianity
2. Islam
3. Secularism
4. Hinduism
5. Buddhism
6. Judaism

The Quran states that Jesus is the Messiah.

Quran 3:45 "The angels proclaimed O Mary Allah gives you good news of a Word from Him his name will be the Messiah".

Muslim scholars have a variety of definitions of the word Messiah. They accept the Jewish beliefs of the coming Messiah[2], but they do not believe that Jesus was the Son of God[3].

The Old Testament is clear that the expected Jewish, prophesied King will come from David's line is actually God, so it is impossible to accept the Jewish prophecies without accepting the Messiahs divinity.

The Old Testament says that the Messiah will be born of a virgin (Isaiah 7:14) in Bethlehem (Micah 5:2), reveal himself around AD 30 (Daniel 9:24-27), die for our sins (Isaiah 53:5-9), yet rise from the dead (Isaiah 53:10-11).

The prophecies make it clear that the Messiah was God.

Isaiah 9:3-7,

*"Nevertheless, there will be no more gloom for those who were in distress. In the past he humbled the land of Zebulun and the land of Naphtali, **but in the future he will honour Galilee of the nations**, by the Way of the Sea, beyond the Jordan—*
[6] **For to us a child is born, to us a son is given**, *and the government will be on his shoulders.*
And he will be called Wonderful Counsellor, Mighty God,
Everlasting Father, Prince of Peace.
[7] *Of the greatness of his government and peace there will be no end.* **He will reign on David's throne** *and over his kingdom, establishing and upholding it with justice and righteousness from that time on and forever."*

The Quran says that the Torah and the Gospels are true (Quran 3:3, Quran 3:48, Quran 5:44, Quran 5:68, Quran 10:94, Quran 28:52). Muslim scholars however say that the Bible has been distorted and isn't the same as the Bible mentioned in the Quran.[4]

But it wouldn't make sense for Muhammad to be speaking about different books when using the word 'Injil' (the Arabic name for the gospel), since it had been a consensus for hundreds of years which books were cannon, and which weren't. Maybe he had a revelation from God with a new meaning of the word Injil, but surely he would have explained that? He would have certainly heard about the Gospels and Torah while living in 7th century Christian Saudi Arabia[5] and it would have been out of context to talk about the Injil and not intend to refer to Matthew, Mark, Luke and John. Similarly, it would be strange to discuss the Torah and not mean the first 5 books of the

Bible, which had been established for even longer.

We have accurate copies of the scriptures dating back to both the time of Muhammad and several centuries earlier. There is very little difference between those early manuscripts and the scriptures that Christians and Jews use in their worship today.

The Dead Sea scrolls confirm that Isaiah (and many other Old Testament books) existed in exactly the form we have it today over 2000 years ago and we have copies of the gospels in the British Library from while Muhammad was still alive. It is clear that these books have not been distorted.

If we accept that Jesus was the Messiah prophesied about by Isaiah, which makes sense, because he was born of a virgin in Bethlehem, he honoured Galilee, he was pierced on a cross, he rose from the dead, none of his bones were broken and he did things that only a God could do, then we must accept that he is who he claims (John 3:16, John 14:6) and put our faith in him as Lord and saviour.

Hinduism believes in reincarnation and karma; we must reach union with Brahman otherwise we will continually reincarnate either as an animal or a human.[6] But we know animals aren't conscious, they aren't capable of storing a human mind in them. If you come back just as an animal/human with a different personality & memories then you aren't the same person and then that means nothing because we can basically say that happens already from a philosophical point of view. They also says that if you try hard enough you can remember your past lives[7], but I think if you try hard enough you will just end up imagining it. It seems more like a philosophy that would be interesting to discuss if you don't really think about the science. Remember this is excluding the fact your brain doesn't transport all your memories to another brain when you die but we are presuming since they believe in lots of Gods they can do it.

Buddhism takes a similar approach, except it does not include any gods.[8] It says you must meditate until you reach true enlightenment and then you can finally die and not be reincarnated but reincarnation can't happen, especially without a deity. Hinduism believes in deities which could be transporting your mind over to new-born babies but if you believe its all left to the power of nature then the philosophy becomes implausible.

But I would also like to point out some problems with the 4 Noble Truths that Buddha laid out. The second Noble truth says that all suffering comes from either greed, ignorance, or hatred. But what about a baby born with a genetic defect which dies within days? The baby has no idea what is going on and it just feels pain. They weren't deluded, their pain was real, the baby wasn't greedy, and it wasn't feeling pain because of its ignorance. The third Noble truth teaches that if we stop having desires we will no longer suffer, but let's imagine for a moment that everyone in the world followed this teaching. Volcanoes would still erupt, there would still be tidal waves, and everyone would still eventually die. There would still be suffering. Humans can't stop pain, suffering and sin ourselves. The fact is, to stop suffering we would need something out of this world.

Jesus was Jewish, in fact Christianity started as a "sect" of Judaism so Judaism shares the (pre-Jesus) Old Testament scriptures with Christianity but not the New Testament. There are Messianic Jews who have accepted Jesus as Messiah, but the majority of Jewish adherents are still waiting for a Messiah, and there are others who see their Jewish identity as a matter of ethnic identity more than a matter of religious belief. If Jesus really rose from the dead when he was crucified on the cross (which I am going to try and prove in my next chapter) then that will provide credibility that Christianity is true and that means that all people should be ready to accept Jesus as Messiah.

It is also important to keep in mind that the Bible has over 40 authors, many eyewitnesses and other historical books that write about it whereas other holy books have only one author so are less credible.

Chapter 6: Proof of Christianity

Many people don't realise there is archaeological evidence for lots of the stuff in the Bible, such as Jericho, the city of Nineveh, Babylon, Ur and the Tower of Babel.[1] The Dead Sea Scrolls from as early as the third Century BC provide copies of nearly the entire Old Testament which has prophecies about Jesus that can also be confirmed.

But the Christian faith hinges on the truth of the resurrection of Jesus because as Paul said *"And if Christ has not been raised, our preaching is useless and so is your faith. More than that, we are then found to be false witnesses about God, for we have testified about God that he raised Christ from the dead. And if Christ has not been raised, your faith is futile; you are still in your sins. [18] Then those also who have fallen asleep in Christ are lost. [19] If only for this life we have hope in Christ, we are of all people most to be pitied."*
1 Corinthians (15:14-18).

Well to start off, we can all agree Jesus was an actual person. Agnostic New Testament scholar and historian, Bart Ehrman says, "Jesus certainly existed, as virtually every competent scholar of antiquity, Christian or non-Christian agrees."[2] There is also more evidence that Jesus existed than Alexander the Great, we have more evidence for Jesus than most of the historical figures in the first century.[3] There are two things that historians believe definitely happened – Jesus' baptism with John the Baptist and the crucifixion.[4]

When Jesus died, a rich man from Arimathea named Joseph paid for his tomb. According to William Lane Craig almost all scholars agree that the tomb was then empty on the third day[5] even though it was guarded by armed roman guards.[6]

How could this have happened without a miracle? Some people believe he just rotted away. But it's not like they would have just mistakenly not seen Jesus' rotting body because there were several people there and when they started preaching about it hundreds of people would have come and check.

Some people claim the tomb was empty because the body was stolen, but there were Roman soldiers stationed outside guarding the tomb. People actually saw him on the third day, and he stayed continuing to preach *in public* for forty days. Why did they steal his body instead of the valuables in the tomb, why did they not reveal his dead body when people started 'lying' he has been raised?

But perhaps it was the disciples who stole his body and then faked it? Well to that I answer: Why would they steal his body? They were mourning their friend that had just died and it wouldn't have been in their nature to do that. They didn't often deceive people and when they did, they felt guilty and apologise for it. The Pharisees had actually thought they might do this:

Matthew (27:63-64): *"They said, 'Sir, we remember what that liar said while he was still alive. He claimed that in three days he would come back from death. ⁶⁴ So please order the tomb to be carefully guarded for three days. If you don't, his disciples may come and steal his body. They will tell the people that he has been raised to life, and this last lie will be worse than the first one.'"*

But what if they lied about him rising? We would realise in that case, and it would be easy to debunk Christianity. Imagine if I went out and said that Michael Jackson had just risen from the dead, no one would believe me! How come the early church didn't quickly fall apart because people realised Jesus didn't really rise from the dead if it was just made up? Wikipedia lists over 28 people who have claimed to be the Davidic Messiah in the last 2000 years[7] and only one of them, Jesus, had followers who claimed that their Messiah rose from the dead.

Gamaliel, a Pharisee, discussed this principle at the time.

Acts 5:36-39,

"Some time ago Theudas appeared, claiming to be somebody, and about four hundred men rallied to him. He was killed, all his followers were dispersed, and it all came to nothing. [37] After him, Judas the Galilean appeared in the days of the census and led a band of people in revolt. He too was killed, and all his followers were scattered. [38] Therefore, in the present case I advise you: Leave these men alone! Let them go! For if their purpose or activity is of human origin, it will fail. [39] But if it is from God, you will not be able to stop these men; you will only find yourselves fighting against God."

If they were making it up why not make themselves the first to meet Jesus after he was resurrected? Instead, it was women who were first to meet Jesus, which would not be the case for anyone making up a story at that time.

Chuck Colson, the White House special counsel during the Watergate scandal said this, "Here were the 10 most powerful men in the United States. With all that power, and we couldn't contain a lie for two weeks. Take it from one who was involved in conspiracy, who saw the frailty of man first-hand. There is no way the 11 apostles, who were with Jesus at the time of the resurrection, could ever have gone around for 40 years proclaiming Jesus' resurrection unless it were true."[8]

The disciples were originally Jews, and they would never make something up like this, it would be highly blasphemous. The Jewish people had stayed faithful under multiple invasions.[9] Making up a story about a crucified man rising from the dead and being the Messiah would not be an acceptable or expected reaction to persecution. If it was a lie, then many of the early Christians really wasted their life because their preaching about Jesus rising from the dead got them killed. At the point of being tortured, surely most of them would have recanted their 'lies' and admitted it was all a fantasy story – they didn't even make any money out of it, it only caused them beatings and suffering.

Maybe Jesus didn't actually die, he just faked it. Well first how did he move the tomb stone, how did he – weak from not eating food or drinking water for 3 days – defeat two armed Roman guards? And the most damning evidence of all, a spear was put into him and when it was pulled out blood and water flowed out (John 19:34); this indicates major blood clotting so he must have died before the spear was put into him, this couldn't have been faked since John wouldn't have known about the significance of it at his time.

What if they went to the wrong tomb? The gospels are careful to point out they specifically went to Jesus'.[10] If they did make a mistake, how come all the other disciples also made the same error and everyone who heard their preaching, who likely would have checked for themselves.

Maybe seeing him afterwards was all just a hallucination. According to the NHS (2021), causes of hallucinations are schizophrenia, alcohol, illegal drugs, or loss of vision.[11] But if you know the disciples, they definitely didn't have schizophrenia, they weren't the type to take excessive alcohol or drugs, and they had good eyesight.

But the biggest evidence against this is that groups of people saw Jesus *at the same time* (Corinthians 15:6) *"After that, he appeared to more than five hundred of the brothers and sisters at the same time, most of whom are still living, though some have fallen asleep."*

And a bit of thinking and research will show a collective hallucination – especially of that size – does not make sense.

Okay okay, how about none of the apostles existed and the New Testament was just written by some guys in AD 200 - years after the Bible says is death of Jesus and all of the apostles? Well, we know James (the brother of Jesus) existed[12], we know John the Baptist existed[13], we know Paul existed[14], we know Herod the Great existed[15], we know Pontius Pilate existed[16], we know Quirinius existed[17], we know Simon Peter existed[18] and the list goes on. So many of the people mentioned in the New Testament are mentioned in extra biblical sources. It's not a myth that was made up, the events in the New Testament can be checked and verified as true. Christians actually existed before AD 200! Nero Caesar killed thousands of Christians after the Great Fire of Rome in AD 64.[19]

But ignoring this, imagining the New Testament was somehow all 'faked' by one person in AD 200, what would his intentions be? Why would he link it to the Old Testament if he wasn't a Jew? Like I said before, coming up with a myth about the Messiah would be major heresy. Jesus was nearly stoned many times for blaspheming and then eventually crucified. Paul was originally a Jew and persecuted many of the early Christians! When he realised Jesus was God though, he himself was persecuted terribly, for example at one point when he went back into Jerusalem the entire city was up in arms and Roman soldiers had to rescue him.

How come the different books had different writing styles? To come up with something like this the author would have had to have been an outcast from society, but then why did the church grow so rapidly with the entire Roman empire becoming Christian by the year AD 313[20], just 100 years after the supposed date of when the New Testament was faked.

What would be the point of a bunch of fake epistles? Was that just when the fake author of the Gospels, who had somehow convinced people into his 'lies' was now counselling people from all over the empire under the names of the 'made up' people from their book?

The New Testament wasn't faked, the apostles existed, Jesus existed and Jesus was really the Son of God. There is no way around it.

We have copies today of Pauls Letters dating back to AD 350 and copies of Johns gospel dating back to as early as AD 125.[21] We have copies of nearly the entire Bible (parts lost due to time) dating back to the beginning of the 4th century.[22] Also, almost all scholars agree most the Pauline epistles were authentic.[23]

1 Thessalonians (which most scholars agree was the first Pauline epistle written) is commonly agreed to be written between AD 49-51.[24] Matthew, Mark, and Luke were written

before the temple was destroyed the second time in AD 70[25] and John was a disciple of Jesus when Jesus was alive (Jesus died between AD 26-33) so the Book of John couldn't have been written long after either. 1 Corinthians 15 quotes a creed about Jesus dying and rising from the dead which most Biblical scholars place at latest *5 years* after Jesus' death! Atheist scholar, Gerd Lüdemann states, "The elements in the tradition are to be dated to the first two years after the crucifixion of Jesus... not later than three years."[26]

Michael Goulder, another atheist scholar, says "[It] goes back at least to what Paul was taught when he was converted, a couple of years after the crucifixion."[27]

Two of the major non-Christian 1st century historians both mention Jesus.

Annals 15.44 (a secular history book, written by Tacitus, a Roman Senator and historian) says:

"Nero fastened the guilt and inflicted the most exquisite tortures on a class hated for their abominations, called Christians by the populace. **Christus, from whom the name had its origin, suffered the extreme penalty during the reign of Tiberius at the hands of one of our procurators, Pontius Pilatus,** and a most mischievous superstition, thus checked for the moment, again broke out not only in Judæa, the first source of the evil, but even in Rome." This means Jesus started Christianity and was really put to death by Pontius Pilate – it wasn't faked.

Antiquities of the Jews 18.3.3 (written by a Jewish historian named Flavius Josephus around AD 93-94)

"About this time there lived Jesus, a wise man, if indeed one ought to call him a man. For he was one who performed surprising deeds and was a teacher of such people as accept the truth gladly. He won over many Jews and many of the Greeks. He was the Christ. And when, upon the accusation of the principal men among us, Pilate had condemned him to a cross, those who had first come to love him did not cease. He appeared to them spending a third day restored to life, for the prophets of God had foretold these things and a thousand other marvels about him. And the tribe of the Christians, so called after him, has still to this day not disappeared."

Some people say the Testimonium Flavianum (Antiquities of the Jews 18.3.3) is a Christian interpolation since a non-Christian would never call Jesus the Christ. But you have to realise, if someone did rise from the dead and tons of people were suddenly saying they were the Messiah, without giving up and falling apart like earlier Messiah claimants, you might just accept it. Also the way he describes Jesus is not at all how a Christian would describe him. A Christian would not call him 'a wise man' (Jesus was more than just wise), 'if indeed one ought to call him a man' (Jesus was fully man and fully God), 'he was one who performed surprising deeds', a Christian wouldn't call his deeds surprising, they normally describe them as miracles. 'And the tribe of the Christians, so called after him, has still to this day not disappeared.' A Christian wouldn't say this because it would be obvious and strange, it sounds like the words of a Jew. It sounds like Josephus thought it was a fact Jesus was the Christ but didn't think it was that important so didn't become a Christian.

Quote from Prof. Darrell Bock, "Jesus isn't just in the Bible. You're talking about over 5,800 Greek manuscripts, over 8,000 Latin manuscripts. Most books that we work with in the ancient world have maybe at best a dozen manuscripts."[28]

Dr. William Lane Craig says most New Testament scholars and historians (including secular ones) believe Jesus really did appear to people after his death one way or another. [29]

Atheist Historian and New Testament scholar Gerd Lüdemann says,
"It may be taken as *historically certain* that Peter and the disciples experiences after Jesus' death in which Jesus appeared to them as the risen Christ"[30]
Lüdemann believes the appearances were just hallucinations, not his literal body.

Craig also points out that James wasn't a Christian while Jesus was alive so why would he become a believer and make up a story about having seen Jesus *after* his death?

More than that, according to Josephus (a first century Jewish historian), James was martyred for his Christian faith. Would you really be willing to be executed because you thought your brother was God?

So, Jesus existed and so did the apostles. The Bible was written before AD 100 and we have copies of books from the New Testament that have survived for us to discover today dating back to as early as the second century. The resurrection makes sense historically and in fact a naturalistic solution *wouldn't make sense*. Jesus' other miracles fit in historically as well. The miracles weren't by chance, Jesus actually claimed to be the Son of God[31] and told us we need to put our trust in Him.[32] The disciples believed Jesus, some wrote about Him, many took him so seriously they were martyred for their faith. All the arguments against Jesus being divine can easily be taken apart. The most rational solution would be to accept what Jesus and His apostles said and put your trust in Him.

Chapter 7: Why does God allow sin?

People often say, Christianity can't be correct because there is suffering, an all powerful and perfect God would get rid of it – or not even create a world with it in the first place in.

It is first important to note that we are made in God's image as conscious beings with free will (see Genesis 1:27)

"So God created mankind in his own image,
   in the image of God he created them;
   male and female he created them."

This means we can make decisions and think. And with that ability comes responsibility, to not sin.[1] Of course God could choose to intervene and stop every sin we do but then we wouldn't have free will so he leaves people to carry on in their sin until Judgement.[2]

But this leaves out the question of natural suffering. Even without humans, the world has suffering. Animals eat each other, tsunamis, tornados, volcanos kill thousands, all earthly lives eventually come to an end.

But God originally created us perfectly as eternal beings that could live happily in the Garden of Eden, but this came to an end when the Devil tempted Adam and Eve to eat the fruit from the tree of knowledge of good and evil – which God had *specifically forbidden* them from eating. When they ate it, they disobeyed God (the first sin) and became self-aware (they realised they were naked[3]). Before this, God had to tell them what was bad such as eating from the tree but now they knew the difference between good and evil.

God then cursed them so they would no longer have eternal life and banished them from the garden into the outside world which had suffering so they couldn't eat from the tree of life

Genesis (3:15)
"By the sweat of your brow
    you will eat your food
until you return to the ground,
    since from it you were taken;
for dust you are
    and to dust you will return."

Genesis (3:22)

"And the LORD God said, 'The man has now become like one of us, knowing good and evil. He must not be allowed to reach out his hand and take also from the tree of life and eat, and live forever.'"

In the story of Joseph and his brothers, Joseph talks about the pain and suffering that he has gone through and says,

Genesis (50:20)

"You intended to harm me, but God intended it for good to accomplish what is now being done, the saving of many lives."

This general principle of God using even the evil works of man and satan to achieve his plans runs throughout the scriptures. Jesus' death on the cross is the ultimate example of satan attempting to destroy God. But God using the situation to destroy sin.

God hasn't ended the world and destroyed evil yet because he has mercy on us. If He destroyed It straight away we would all be destroyed and go to Hell since we are sinful. So, He is giving everyone time to put their faith in Him.[4]

Now there is suffering, but if we put our trust in Jesus Christ as our Lord and Saviour He will atone for our sins so we won't be sent to Hell. God hasn't eliminated sin yet, He is giving us all a chance but judgement day is coming.

Chapter 8: Why do people go to Hell?

First let's imagine you created the world and you see people sinning, people driving planes into buildings, people committing mass genocides and waging huge wars. There should be a punishment. But an omnibenevolent God would just forgive sin, wouldn't he? Jesus teaches people to turn another cheek, rather than taking an eye for an eye (Matthew 5:38-39).

Well, this brings us to the devil. Most biblical scholars say he was originally one of God's top angels but then he got jealous and betrayed God. God is perfectly just and so He could not let it slide. satan was banished into Hell which was void of all things good.[1]

Ezekiel (28:12-15):

You were the seal of perfection,
    full of wisdom and perfect in beauty.
[13] You were in Eden,
    the garden of God;
every precious stone adorned you:
    [14] You were anointed as a guardian cherub,
    for so I ordained you.
You were on the holy mount of God;
    you walked among the fiery stones.
[15] You were blameless in your ways
    from the day you were created
    till wickedness was found in you.
So I drove you in disgrace from the mount of
God,
    and I expelled you, guardian cherub,
    from among the fiery stones.

We are also sinful[2], we all deserve to be sent to
Hell.[3] We can't save ourselves since we aren't
perfect. God can't just forget about our sins
since then He would be unjust, God didn't want

us to all go to Hell though since he was all merciful.

Up to now we were talking about God the Father, this now brings us to Jesus.

Jesus who is the Word or Logos is God.[4] He is the Son, He wasn't created, He always existed, He was begotten.[5] Jesus volunteered to go into the world as a sacrifice for our sins. He was perfect and a man. This means He could take the blame for mankind's sins. Jesus died on a cross for the sins of all of mankind, who can accept his offer of eternal life by putting their trust in him. Death has no dominion over God.

If we repent and put our trust in Jesus as our Lord, Saviour and Christ, sent by God the Father, who died then rose from the dead. We can be saved from our sins.[6]

John 3:16
"For God so loved the world that he gave his one and only Son, that whoever believes in him shall not perish but have eternal life."

John 3:36

"Whoever believes in the Son has eternal life; whoever does not obey the Son shall not see life, but the wrath of God remains on him"

James 1:2-6

"Consider it pure joy, my brothers and sisters, whenever you face trials of many kinds, because you know that the testing of your faith produces perseverance. Let perseverance finish its work so that you may be mature and complete, not lacking anything. If any of you lacks wisdom, you should ask God, who gives generously to all without finding fault, and it will be given to you. But when you ask, you must believe and not doubt, because the one who doubts is like a wave of the sea, blown and tossed by the wind."

Notes:

Introduction:

1. Irreligion is now the 3rd biggest religion, see:
https://www.pewresearch.org/fact-tank/2017/04/05/christians-remain-worlds-largest-religious-group-but-they-are-declining-in-europe/
2. Humanism is taught in school in the UK, see:
https://humanists.international/2021/03/humanism-officially-enters-in-school-curriculum-in-wales/ from the age of 5, see:
https://www.telegraph.co.uk/education/educationnews/10396977/Lessons-in-humanism-from-age-five-in-new-RE-lessons.html
3. 390,197 people believe in the Jedi Knight religion UK, see:
https://web.archive.org/web/20030401182751/http://www.statistics.gov.uk/census2001/profiles/rank/jedi.asp/
4. 100,000 humanists in the UK. In the "More about us" section of https://humanism.org.uk/about/ or
https://web.archive.org/web/20210209124521/https://humanism.org.uk/about/
5. 45% of UK scientists are atheists, see: https://www.futurity.org/uk-scientists-less-religious-1937692-2/
6. Isaac Newton was a Christian, see: https://en.wikipedia.org/wiki/Religious_views_of_Isaac_Newton
7. James Maxwell was a Christian, see:
https://en.wikipedia.org/w/index.php?title=James_Clerk_Maxwell&oldid=1029958095 or
https://web.archive.org/web/20121231001816/http://silas.psfc.mit.edu/maxwell/
8. Michael Faraday was a Christian, see
https://www.asa3.org/ASA/PSCF/1991/PSCF6-91Eichman.html

9. Charles Babbage was a Christian. Quote from Charles Babbage "My excellent mother taught me the usual forms of my daily and nightly prayer; and neither in my father nor my mother was there any mixture of bigotry and intolerance on the one hand, nor on the other of that unbecoming and familiar mode of addressing the Almighty which afterwards so much disgusted me in my youthful years." See https://en.wikisource.org/wiki/Passages_from_the_Life_of_a_Philosopher/Chapter_II#8 another quote "I may now state, as the result of a long life spent in studying the works of the Creator, that I am satisfied they afford far more satisfactory and more convincing proofs of the existence of a supreme Being than any evidence transmitted through human testimony can possibly supply."

10. Albert Einstein was a Deist, he did not believe in a personal God like Abrahamic religions. Quote: "It was, of course, a lie what you read about my religious convictions, a lie which is being systematically repeated. I do not believe in a personal God and I have never denied this but have expressed it clearly." See: Albert Einstein, the Human Side: New Glimpses from His Archives, by Albert Einstein, Page 43, 1972. Einstein was not an atheist "In view of such harmony in the cosmos which I, with my limited human mind, am able to recognize, there are yet people who say there is no God. But what really makes me angry is that they quote me for the support of such views."

"The fanatical atheists...are like slaves who are still feeling the weight of their chains which they have thrown off after hard struggle. They are creatures who—in their grudge against the traditional opium of the people—cannot hear the music of spheres." Both quotes here are from https://web.archive.org/web/20070509111721/http://www.time.com/time/magazine/article/0,9171,1607298-3,00.html

He wasn't a pantheist either "I'm not an atheist. I don't think I can call myself a pantheist."
https://web.archive.org/web/20070509002926/http://www.time.com/time/magazine/article/0,9171,1607298-2,00.html

It seems like he believes in a creator God as well from this quote "The child knows someone must have written those books. It does not know how." (from the same link)

So it seems he is a Deist (believes in an impersonal creator God).

11. Thomas Edison was a Deist. Quote "I do not believe in the God of the theologians; but that there is a Supreme Intelligence I do not doubt." Quote from https://quotefancy.com/quote/916706/Thomas-A-Edison-I-do-not-believe-in-the-God-of-the-theologians-but-that-there-is-a

12. Max Planck was a Deist. He believed in a creator God "As a man who has devoted his whole life to the most clearheaded science, to the study of matter, I can tell you as a result of my research about the atoms this much: There is no matter as such! All matter originates and exists only by virtue of a force which brings the particles of an atom to vibration and holds this most minute solar system of the atom together. . . . We must assume behind this force the existence of a conscious and intelligent Mind. This Mind is the matrix of all matter." See https://www.goodreads.com/quotes/7819522-as-a-man-who-has-devoted-his-whole-life-to for quote

Max Planck didn't believe in a personal God like the Abrahamic religions though "[I do not believe] in a personal God, let alone a Christian God." See https://www.goodreads.com/quotes/953497-i-do-not-believe-in-a-personal-god-let-alone for quote.

13. Charles Darwin was a Deist, quote "I have never been an atheist in the sense of denying the existence of a God." See https://www.darwinproject.ac.uk/letter/DCP-LETT-12041.xml

He also believed in a creator God Quote "Nevertheless you have expressed my inward conviction, though far more vividly and clearly than I could have done, that the Universe is not the result of chance." See https://web.archive.org/web/20160306181124/https://www.darwinproject.ac.uk/letter/DCP-LETT-13230.xml

14. https://quoteinvestigator.com/2011/12/16/spirit-manifest/

15. https://quotefancy.com/quote/762889/Albert-Einstein-The-more-I-study-science-the-more-I-believe-in-God

Chapter 1:

1. See 11:00-11:20 of this video
https://www.youtube.com/watch?v=OVEuQg_Mglw&t=690s
2. https://quotefancy.com/quote/966530/Richard-Dawkins-Faith-is-belief-without-evidence-and-reason-coincidentally-that-s-also
and https://web.archive.org/web/20121030144700/http://www.thehumanist.org/humanist/articles/dawkins.html
3. https://www.space.com/20330-cosmic-microwave-background-explained-infographic.html
4. *The Grand Design* by Stephen Hawking, 2010, Page 180,
5. *The Intelligent Universe*, by Fred Hoyle, 1983, Page 17
6. *The Emperor's New Mind*, by Roger Penrose, 1989, Page 383
7. Occam's Razor or Ockham's Razor - "entities should not be multiplied beyond necessity". The multiverse theory is the ultimate example of this, it multiplies this universe by *infinite* without necessity.
8. Quote is from https://philosophynow.org/issues/46/Newtons_Flaming_Laser_Sword
9. The Inverse Gambler's Fallacy: The Argument from Design. The Anthropic Principle Applied to Wheeler Universes, by Ian Hacking, 1989. https://www.jstor.org/stable/2254310
10. https://www.newscientist.com/article/mg23331133-200-universes-that-spawn-cosmic-brains-should-go-on-the-scrapheap/ and https://www.newscientist.com/article/mg22229692-600-quantum-twist-could-kill-off-the-multiverse/
11. *The Return of The God Hypothesis*, by Stephen Meyer, 2021, Page 340-341
12. "Eventually, entire virtual worlds will be created inside computers, their conscious inhabitants unaware that they are the simulated products of somebody else's technology. For every original world, there will be a stupendous number of available virtual worlds -- some of which would even include machines simulating virtual worlds of their own, and so on ad infinitum. Taking the multiverse theory at face value, therefore, means accepting that virtual worlds are more numerous

than 'real' ones ... Far from doing away with a transcendent Creator, the multiverse theory actually injects that very concept at almost every level of its logical structure." See https://www.nytimes.com/2003/04/12/opinion/a-brief-history-of-the-multiverse.html

13. http://hyperphysics.phy-astr.gsu.edu/hbase/Astro/planck.html or http://abyss.uoregon.edu/~js/cosmo/lectures/lec20.html or Spontaneous creation of the universe from nothing, by Dongshan He, Dongfeng Gao, and Qing-yu Cai. https://arxiv.org/pdf/1404.120 7.pdf

14. https://www.newscientist.com/question/how-did-life-begin/

15. https://www.frontiersin.org/articles/10.3389/fpsyg.2018.01537/full I recommend *Mind and Cosmos*, by Thomas Nagel, 2012, if you are interested in this subject.

16. https://starchild.gsfc.nasa.gov/docs/StarChild/questions/question 30.html#:~:text=We%20don't%20really%20know.&text=However%2C%20if%20we%20are%20to,two%20bodies%2C%20any%20two%20particles.

17. https://www.sciencemag.org/news/2021/03/ancient-earth-was-water-world

18. https://www.sciencemag.org/news/2018/02/land-plants-arose-earlier-thought-and-may-have-had-bigger-impact-evolution-animals or https://www.newscientist.com/article/dn21417-first-land-plants-plunged-earth-into-ice-age/

19. https://www.livescience.com/oldest-green-algae-discovered.html

20. https://www.nature.com/articles/d41586-018-06767-6

21. https://www.guinnessworldrecords.com/world-records/first-land-animal

22. The book of Revelation has letters to the Seven Churches (Revelation 2-3), the Seven Seals (Revelation 6:1, Revelation 8:1), Seven Trumpets (Revelation 8:2), Seven Bowls (Revelation 16), Seven Angels (Revelation 8:2) and probably the best example is the Sevenfold Spirit (Revelation 1:4, 3:1, 4:5, and 5:6). Whereas satan or the mark of the beast is represented by 666 (Revelation 13:8) which is incomplete, or imperfect compared to 7 which is complete and perfect.

23. For the number six and seven being symbolic see *The City of God*, by Augustine, Book XI, Chapter 30-31

For the days being symbolic see: *Literal Meaning of* Genesis, By Augustine, Book V, Chapter 2

For us not being able to understand see: "Those days... are beyond the experience and knowledge of us mortal earthbound men." *The Literal Meaning of* Genesis, By Augustine, Book IV, Chapter 27

24. *Literal Meaning of Genesis*, by Augustine, Book V: (Chapter 7, Paragraph 20), (Chapter 7, Paragraph 22), (Chapter 20, Paragraph 41), (Chapter 23, Paragraph 45), and (Chapter 23, Paragraph 44) "[God] created all [creates] together... whose visible forms He produces through the ages"

25. *Irenaeus against Heresies*, by Irenaeus, Book V, Chapter 23

26. The Epic of Gilgamesh, written in 2100 BC, is one of Mesopotamia's accounts of Noah's flood. The Epic of Enuma Elish, written between the 6th and the 12th century BC, is a Babylonian account on creation. The epic of Atra-Hasis, written in the 18th century BC, is a Babylonian account on creation and Noah's flood. The Eridu Genesis, written in 1600 BC, is a Sumerian account on creation and Noah's flood. The Epic of Lugalbanda, written between the 18th and 21st century BC, is a Sumerian epic about the King of Uruk. The Epic of Enmerkar and the Lord of Aratta, written in the 21st century BC, is a Sumerian account of conflicts between 2 kings. It also talks about confusions of tongues and building a tower so has been compared to the Tower of Babel.

27. God was communicating to humanity with our current knowledge of the world. It was not God's intention to teach us that the earth was an ellipsoid surrounded by stars thousands of light years away. Similarly, if He came to us right now, He would communicate using our contemporary knowledge. We would be confused if He came to us with 41st century science. At that point the Hebrews thought the earth was flat, the sky was a firmament with stars in and it had another ocean on top. They would have been confused if God came to them with 21st century science. God had no intention to come to them with 21st century science, He wanted to teach them about Him, that he created

the universe. We know their cosmology is incorrect since science has advanced, just because God communicated to them using it doesn't mean we have to believe it.

28. *The Goldilocks Enigma: Why is the Universe Just Right for Life?*, by Paul Davies, 2007, Page 5

29. https://homepages.spa.umn.edu/~larry/CLASS/CATASTROPHE/anthropic.html

Chapter 2

1. https://www.azquotes.com/quote/683815

2. https://www.cslewisinstitute.org/webfm_send/4674 or https://www.cslewisinstitute.org/Science_and_Faith_Friendly_Allies_Not_Hostile_Enemies_page4

Chapter 3

1. https://www.goodreads.com/quotes/1030054-eventually-i-believe-current-attempts-to-understand-the-mind-by 2

2. http://web.archive.org/web/20160306181124/https://www.darwinproject.ac.uk/letter/DCP-LETT-13230.xml

3. the universe is 436,117,076,640,000,000 seconds old, see https://81018.com/formulas/#1b

4. https://math.stackexchange.com/questions/2049714/can-something-be-statistically-impossible#:~:text=4%20Answers&text=A%20statistical%20impossibility%20is%20a,in%20a%20rational%2C%20reasonable%20argument.

5. https://en.wikipedia.org/wiki/Junkyard_tornado

6. Conclusion to *The Mind of God,* by Paul Davies, 1992

7. https://www.goodreads.com/quotes/4109864-whatever-one-may-think-about-the-possibility-of-a-designer

8. https://www.discovermagazine.com/planet-earth/which-ancient-city-is-considered-the-oldest-in-the-world

9. http://www.ecifm.rdg.ac.uk/history.htm#:~:text=First%20human%20farmers%3A%20about%2012%2C000%20years%20ago.&text=Some%20of%20the%20food%20gathering,gatherer%20societies%20were%2

0relatively%20advanced.&text=Cultivation%20involves%20the%20delib
erate%20sowing,necessarily%20differ%20from%20wild%20populations

10. "Writing was invented independently in at least four different times and places: Mesopotamia, Egypt, China, and Mesoamerica. Of these original writing systems, Egyptian and Sumerian are the oldest known. The earliest evidence of phonetic writing in Egypt dates to about 3250 BC; the earliest known complete sentence in the Egyptian language has been dated to about 2690 BC. Egypt's Copts used the spoken language until the late seventeenth century AD, making it one of history's longest surviving recorded languages." Quote from:
https://www.oxfordhandbooks.com/view/10.1093/oxfordhb/97801999
35413.001.0001/oxfordhb-9780199935413-e-61

11. Genesis 2:14 says that 2 of the rivers leading from the Garden were the Tigris and Euphrates, we know the location of these rivers today to be Mesopotamia (or Iraq).

12. https://www.history.com/topics/pre-history/neolithic-revolution
The Neolithic revolution started in the Fertile Crescent (West Asia)

13. "Civilizations first appeared in Mesopotamia (what is now Iraq) and later in Egypt." https://www.nationalgeographic.org/article/key-components-civilization/

14. If you add up the years in Genesis 5 from you get the number 1656

15. https://www.discovermagazine.com/planet-earth/biblical-type-floods-are-real-and-theyre-absolutely-enormous

16. http://www.ecifm.rdg.ac.uk/history.htm#:~:text=First%20human%2
0farmers%3A%20about%2012%2C000%20years%20ago.&text=Some%
20of%20the%20food%20gathering,gatherer%20societies%20were%20r
elatively%20advanced.&text=Cultivation%20involves%20the%20deliber
ate%20sowing,necessarily%20differ%20from%20wild%20populations.

Chapter 4

1. https://www.sciencealert.com/humanity-hasn-t-reached-as-far-into-space-as-you-think

2. https://exoplanets.nasa.gov/discovery/exoplanet-catalog/

3. https://www.veritasgenetics.com/our-thinking/whole-story/

4. See *Rare Earth: Why Complex Life Is Uncommon in the Universe* by Peter Douglas Ward & Donald Brownlee, 2000

5. Ibid.

6. George Gaylord Simpson summarized the search for extraterrestrial life—and more particularly intelligent life as "a gamble of the most adverse odds in history." This View of Life: The World of an Evolutionist by George Simpson.

7. "Even if there were intelligent extraterrestrial life, and even if it had developed a highly sophisticated technology, the timing of their efforts and those of our engineers would have to overlap to an altogether improbable degree, considering the amounts of astronomical time available. Every aspect of 'Extraterrestrial Intelligence' that we consider confronts us with astronomically low probabilities. If one multiplies them together, one comes out so close to zero, that it is zero for all extents and purposes.". The Probability of Extraterrestrial Life, By Ernst Mayr (1985)

8. https://muse.jhu.edu/article/406404

9. Quote is from, https://www.space.com/origin-of-life-rna-universe-model.html

Prof. Totani's paper is at: https://www.nature.com/articles/s41598-020-58060-0?utm_medium=affiliate&utm_source=commissio n_junction&utm_campaign=3_nsn6445_deeplink_PID100052171&utm _content=deeplink

10. https://www.goodreads.com/en/book/show/1844214.Do_Animal s_Think_#:~:text=program%20your%20computer%3F,In%20this%20pro vocative%20book%2C%20noted%20animal%20expert%20Clive%20Wyn ne%20debunks,the%20same%20way%20we%20do.

11. See 1:26:06-1:26:10 of https://www.youtube.com/watch?v=5OXPlUCGScY&t=5171s

12. *The Tao of Physics* by Fritjof Capra, 1975, Page 126

Chapter 5

1. https://www.pewresearch.org/fact-tank/2017/04/05/christians-remain-worlds-largest-religious-group-but-they-are-declining-in-europe/

2. "Muslims accept the Jewish belief that there were prophecies about the coming of the Messiah." https://aboutislam.net/counseling/ask-about-islam/what-is-the-meaning-of-messiah/

3. "Muslims however deny the Christian belief that Jesus was the Son of God" https://aboutislam.net/counseling/ask-about-islam/what-is-the-meaning-of-messiah/

4. Quote from Abdullah Yusuf Ali, "The Injil (Greek, Evangel equals Gospel) spoken of by the Qur'an is not the New Testament. It is not the four Gospels now received as canonical. It is the single Gospel which, Islam teaches, was revealed to Jesus, and which he taught. Fragments of it survive in the received canonical Gospels and in some others, of which traces survive (e.g., the Gospel of Childhood or the Nativity, the Gospel of St.Barnabas, etc.)." Quote is from: https://archive.org/details/in.ernet.dli.2015.135657/page/n350/mode/2up

5. Muhammad was born in 570 and started preaching when he was 40 so in 610 (in the 7th Century). Saudi Arabia was predominantly Christian at that point.

6. https://www.history.com/topics/religion/hinduism

7. https://www.jstor.org/stable/23447913

8. https://www.history.com/topics/religion/buddhism

Chapter 6

1. A large ziggurat called Etemenanki was rebuilt by Nabopolassar and Nebuchadnezzar II sometime in the seventh and sixth century, you can still see the remains of it today. The original though was built thousands of years before. Foundation cylinders with inscriptions from Nabopolassar were found in the 1880s which read "At that time my lord Marduk [a Babylonian god] told me in regard to Etemenanki, **the ziqqurrat of Babylon,** *which before my day was already very weak and*

badly buckled, to ground its bottom on the breast of the netherworld, to make its top vie with the heavens." See: https://eprints.soas.ac.uk/3858/2/TowerOfBabel.AfO.pdf (Page 15) Nabopolassar said himself that he was rebuilding the original Tower of Babel.

2. *Writing in the Name of God*, by Bart Ehrman, 2012, Page 285

3. Unlike today where everyone living in a developed country will have hundreds of documents about them, in the first century it would be extremely rare to have as many as 6 documents concerning you. That is if you are famous, if you were an average person or lower then you probably wouldn't have any. So for a peasant who suffered the death of a slave – crucifixion – to get more primary/secondary literary mentions (within a reasonable amount of time after his death, ~80-150 years) than the emperor of his time (Tiberius) is crazy. See http://web.archive.org/web/20101110025007/http://www.preventingt ruthdecay.org/dje.shtml Alexander The Great died in 323 BC and he didn't have any biographies written on him until first century Rome.

4. *Jesus Remembered*, by James D. G. Dunn, 2003 Page 339. "The historicity of the baptism and crucifixion of Jesus command almost universal assent rank so high on the almost impossible to doubt or deny scale of historical facts"

5. https://www.reasonablefaith.org/writings/scholarly-writings/historical-jesus/the-historicity-of-the-empty-tomb-of-jesus/

6. https://www.reasonablefaith.org/writings/scholarly-writings/historical-jesus/the-guard-at-the-tomb/

7. https://en.wikipedia.org/wiki/List_of_messiah_claimants

8. https://www.goodreads.com/quotes/555921-i-know-the-resurrection-is-a-fact-and-watergate-proved

9. Jews stayed faithful to the Lord resisting paganism throughout history, when the Assyrians invaded Israel in 722 BC, Judah was invaded in 600 BC by Babylon, then fell to Persian rule in 539 BC and was conquered in 323 BC by Alexander the Great. In the book of Daniel, he and his friends continued to worship the Lord when they were

threatened with death and were thrown in a fiery furnace and a lion's den but survived with God's help. King Nebuchadnezzar II was so amazed he worshiped Daniel's God (Daniel 3:28) as did the Persian King Darius (Daniel 6:26). Around that time the Babylonian/Persians started worshiping a monotheistic god instead of polytheistic gods. Zoroastrianism started at this time. "The Iranian prophet and religious reformer Zarathustra (flourished before the 6th century BCE)... Darius I (522–486) and his successors worshipped Auramazda (Ahura Mazdā)" quote from https://www.britannica.com/topic/Zoroastrianism

10 See Matthew 28:1-2 they (Mary and Mary Magdalene) went to the tomb and an angel was there on it and rolled the tombstone away. An angel wouldn't have been there on the wrong tomb talking about Jesus on the wrong tomb. See Mark 16:6 they see an angel inside of the tomb (the stone had already been rolled away) talking about Jesus, why would this happen if it was the wrong tomb? See Luke 24:2-6 the same as Mark. John 20:2 Mary Magdalene (not Mary, Jesus' mother) saw the tomb was empty, so they went and got Peter and John. John 20:5 they see that Jesus was not there, just the cloth. John 20:11 Mary Magdalene is crying outside the tomb when John 20:12 she sees 2 angels, John 20:14-15 she turns around and sees Jesus.

11. hhttps://www.nhs.uk/mental-health/feelings-symptoms-behaviours/feelings-and-symptoms/hallucinations-hearing-voices/

12. Antiquities of the Jews, Book 20, Chapter 9. By Flavius Josephus http://www.perseus.tufts.edu/hopper/text?doc=J.+AJ+20.9.1

13. Antiquities of the Jews, Book 18, Chapter 5. By Flavius Josephus http://www.perseus.tufts.edu/hopper/text?doc=J.%20AJ%2018.5&lang =original

14. 2 Peter 3:15–16

15. Antiquities of the Jews, Book 15, Chapter 1. By Josephus Flavius http://penelope.uchicago.edu/josephus/ant-15.html

16. https://www.independent.co.uk/news/people/historical-notes-pontius-pilate-name-set-stone-1084786.html

17. Antiquities of the Jews, Book 18, Chapter 1

18. first epistle to the Corinthians by Clement
https://www.newadvent.org/fathers/1010.htm

19. Annals 15.41-44 "Nero fastened the guilt **and inflicted the most exquisite tortures** on a class hated for their abominations, **called Christians** by the populace."

20. https://www.pbs.org/empires/romans/empire/christians.html#:~:text=In%20313%20AD%2C%20the%20Emperor,religion%20of%20the%20Roman%20Empire.

21. https://biblearchaeologyreport.com/2019/02/15/the-earliest-new-testament-manuscripts/

22. Codex Sinaiticus which contains nearly the entire New and Old Testament dates back to AD 330-360, See https://www.bl.uk/collection-items/codex-sinaiticus and the Codex Vaticanus was written between AD 300-325, See https://en.m.wikipedia.org/wiki/Codex_Vaticanus

23. "There is nearly universal consensus in modern New Testament scholarship on a core group of authentic Pauline epistles whose authorship is rarely contested: Romans, 1 and 2 Corinthians, Galatians, Philippians, 1 Thessalonians, and Philemon." https://en.wikipedia.org/w/index.php?title=Authorship_of_the_Pauline_epistles&oldid=1034130429

24. https://www.esv.org/resources/esv-global-study-bible/introduction-to-1-thessalonians/

25. Each of the first three Gospels contains predictions by Jesus concerning the destruction of Jerusalem and the Temple (Matthew 24; Mark 13; Luke 21), but none records the fulfilment so the first gospels can be estimated to be written before AD 70.

Acts ends with Paul alive (Acts 28:31), Paul died in AD 67 but mentioned Paul's appeal to Ceased in AD 57-60 so it can be estimated that the book of Acts was written in AD 62. We know the book of Luke was written before Acts so that means Luke was written before AD 60. Mark is believed to be written before Luke and according to the early church Matthew was the first gospel written in AD 41 so Mark was probably written sometime in the fifties. See https://www.blueletterbible.org/Comm/stewart_don/faq/historical-accuracy-of-the-bible/question10-when-were-the-gospels-written.cfm

26. *The Resurrection of Jesus*, by Gerd Lüdemann, 1994, Page 38

27. *The Baseless Fabric of a Vision*, By Michael Goulder, 1996, Page 48

28. https://www1.cbn.com/cbnnews/us/2017/april/why-you-can-believe-in-the-resurrection

29. See 19:58 https://youtu.be/Z8lkuuhVkOl

30. https://www.goodreads.com/quotes/7474306-atheistic-new-testament-scholar-gerd-ludemann-concludes-it-may-be

31. John 5:18

32. John 3:16

Chapter 7

1. 1 John 2:1

2. Romans 1:21-24, Revelation 22:11

3. Genesis 3:7

4. 2 Peter 3:9

Chapter 8

1. 2 Peter 2:4, Revelation 12:9, Ezekiel 28:13-19

2. Romans 3:23, 1 John 1:8

3 Romans 6:23

4. Jesus is The Word (or Logos) and God, see John 1:1-3. Jesus is also called God in Titus 2:13, Jesus is called God, 2 Peter 1:1, Jesus is called God, John 20:28 Thomas calls Jesus God and Jesus endorses him

5. Hebrews 1:5 and Hebrews 5:5 describe Jesus as begotten. In Revelation 22:13 it is Jesus speaking (see Revelation 22:16) and He says "I am the Alpha and the Omega, the first and the last, the beginning and the end." If he was the First, He couldn't have been created.

6. John 3:16, John 3:36, John 17:3, John 17:18, John 17:21, Mark 1:15, 1 John 1:9, Acts 2:38, Romans 10:9

Printed in Great Britain
by Amazon